THE BIG BOOK OF CLIMBING

tra.publishing

XIMO ABADÍA

AN ILLUSTRATED HISTORY OF MOUNTAINEERING, BOULDERING, AND BEYOND

TABLE OF CONTENTS

CLIMBING	04
TRADITIONAL CLIMBING	22
SPORT CLIMBING	32
BOULDERING	42
SOLO CLIMBING	50
FREE BASE	50
URBAN CLIMBING	51
PSICOBLOC	51
TOKYO 2020	52
CLIMBING WALLS	54
PARACLIMBING	56
CLIMBING SUSTAINABILITY	58
THE PIONEERS	60
GLOSSARY	62

CLIMBING

Whether you are climbing the face of a rock, climbing the rock wall in a gym, or climbing a sheet of ice, getting to the top is demanding. Mastering climbing requires more than technical knowledge.

It involves a series of possible dangers such as avalanches, adverse weather conditions, lack of oxygen, and complex descents that can be fatal.

The fourteen highest peaks in the world are above 26,657 feet (or 8,000 meters) and are known to International Mountaineering and Climbing Federation as "the 8,000s."

HISTORY

The first records of alpine climbing date back to the 6th century, when shepherds in the valleys of the Alps nailed horseshoes to the soles of their boots and went up the frozen mountains with their flocks. As the years went by and British tourists arrived, many of those shepherds became mountain guides.

On August 8, 1786, the first climb was historically recorded. **Jacques Balmat** and **Michel-Gabriel Paccard** climbed to the top of Mont Blanc (15,781 feet/810 meters) for the first time to observe what a barometer would do at that elevation.

Marie Paradis, the first woman to reach the summit of Mont Blanc, on July 14, 1808, is recognized as the first female mountaineer.

On July 14, 1865, **Edward Whymper** was the first to reach the summit of the Matterhorn (14,692 feet/4,478 meters) in the Italian-Swiss Alps. During the descent, four of the Englishmen who were part of the expedition died. One of the climbing team who lost his life was a knight of the British court, so Queen Victoria considered banning mountaineering.

English climber **Albert Mummery** began climbing without a guide, which was more risky. He was part of the first expedition to Nanga Parbat (26,657 feet/8,125 meters). He and his entire team later died on August 24, 1895, in an avalanche while trying to find another route to climb the same mountain.

En 1908, **Annie Peck**, an American professor, mountaineer, and suffragist, reached the summit of Huascarán, in the Peruvian Andes, and became the first woman to conquer a mountain peak of more than 6,000 meters (19,685 feet). Three years later, she reached the summit of Coropuna (6,377 meters/20,922 feet). When she reached the top, she placed a banner that read "Votes for Women."

The English climber **George Mallory** was a part of the first three expeditions that attempted to conquer Everest. On June 9, 1924, he disappeared along with his teammate, **Andrew Irvine**, at more than 26,247 feet (8,000 meters) above sea level. Even today, we don't know if they managed to reach the summit. The secret may be recorded in Mallory's Kodak Model B camera, which has not been found.

Two of the most outstanding figures in the history of mountaineering were the innovative French mountaineers and mountain guides **Lionel Terray** and **Gaston Rébuffat**. Friends and teammates, they were the first to attempt numerous more technically challenging first ascents. In 1950, they played an important role in the French expedition to Annapurna.

Lionel Terray's teammate, the French mountaineer and experienced mountain guide **Louis Lachenal**, was one of the most important climbing figures after the Second World War. He and Terray succeeded in their attempts of seemingly impossible climbs with incredible ease and speed. Lachenal, together with another legend, the French mountaineer **Maurice Herzog**, became the first to reach 26,657 feet (8,000 meters) on Annapurna.

Polish climber **Wanda Rutkiewicz** was the first woman to summit K2 and the first European woman to reach the summit of Everest. She was also the lead of an all-female team, which was revolutionary at that time. She died on the mountain, less than three hundred meters from reaching another eight thousand (26,657 feet), the Kangchenjunga.

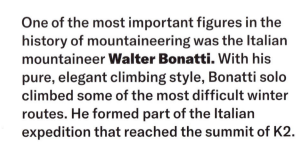

One of the most important figures in the history of mountaineering was the Italian mountaineer **Walter Bonatti.** With his pure, elegant climbing style, Bonatti solo climbed some of the most difficult winter routes. He formed part of the Italian expedition that reached the summit of K2.

Another figure who changed the history of mountaineering was the Austrian climber **Hermann Buhl**. On July 3, 1953, ignoring the orders of his expedition leader, he reached the summit of Nanga Parbat alone and without oxygen. He left his ice ax at the top as proof of his success, thus making going back down the mountain even more difficult.

On July 16, 1975, Japanese mountaineer **Junko Tabei** was the first woman to reach the summit of Everest on an all-female expedition.

On September 18, 1987, Polish climber **Jerzy Kukuczka** became the second person to complete the summits of the fourteen highest mountains on the planet. He stood out for his clean, creative, and confident style.

The Italian climber **Reinhold Messner**, considered by many the most important figure in mountaineering, made it to the summit of the fourteen highest mountains and changed the history of the eight-thousands forever.

11

THE FOURTEEN HIGHEST PEAKS

The term eight thousand (note that this is referring to meters) indicates the fourteen highest mountains in the world. Eight thousand meters is a dramatic 26,657 feet above sea level! All of the highest peaks are located on the Asian continent, specifically, in the Himalayas and Karakoram mountain ranges. In 1895, an attempt was made for the first time to reach one of these fourteen summits, but that expedition to the top of Nanga Parbat failed, and three of the climbing team died in an avalanche.

From seven thousand five hundred meters (24,606 feet) you enter the so-called **DEATH ZONE.** Human life is not possible for long because the low atmospheric pressure at that altitude prevents the absorption of oxygen when breathing. That is why mountaineers trying to climb higher that that carry and (usually) use oxygen.

On June 3, 1950, **Maurice Herzog** and **Louis Lachenal** reached the summit of Annapurna and became the first to summit a mountain of more than eight thousand meters. **Lionel Terray**, **Gaston Rébuffat,** and the *Sherpa Adjiba* gave up trying to reach the summit themselves in order to help Lachenal and Herzog on their descent. Both climbers suffered frostbite so badly that they ended up losing parts of their fingers and toes.

On October 16, 1986, Italian mountaineer **Reinhold Messner** was the first person to complete the ascent of all fourteen eight-thousanders without using oxygen.

In May 2010, the Spanish climber **Edurne Pasaban** became the first woman to summit all fourteen of the eight-thousanders.

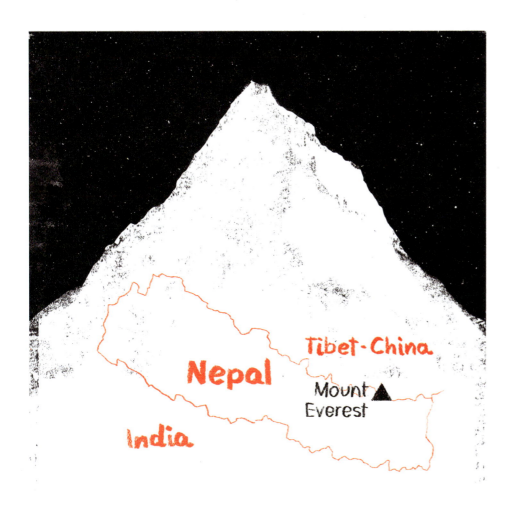

Located in the Himalayan mountain range (in the Mahalangur Himal submountain range) on the border between China and Nepal, and with an altitude of 29,029 feet (8,848 meters), **EVEREST** is the highest mountain in the world. More than three hundred people have lost their lives trying to climb to the top.

Mount Everest was named after the British geographer and surveyor **George Everest**, but Everest himself didn't think it was right to name "the roof of the world" after his name.

On May 29, 1953, climbing the Nepalese slope, the New Zealander **Edmund Hillary** and the Nepalese *Sherpa* **Tenzing Norgay** were the first mountaineers to successfully reach the summit of Mount Everest.

On May 16, 1975, the Japanese mountaineer **Junko Tabei**, summited it, by climbing the same route that Hillary and Norgay had taken. Days later, on May 27, the Tibetan climber, **Phantog** climbed to the summit using the more demanding route of the North Face.

In 1978, **Reinhold Messner** and the **Austrian Peter** Habeler were the first to summit Mount Everest without using oxygen. In 1980, Messner repeated the climb alone.

In 2020, Spanish climber **Kilian Jornet** reached the summit of Everest without using oxygen in just ten hours.

13

Located in the Karakoram Mountain range, in the Himalayas, at 8,611 meters (28,251 feet), **K2** is the second highest mountain on the planet and the peak that presents the most technical difficulties when climbing.

On July 31, 1954, Italian climbers **Lino Lacedelli** and **Achille Compagnoni** were the first to reach the summit without oxygen.
Both blamed the mountaineering legend **Walter Bonatti** for using up the expedition's oxygen and making it necessary for them to complete the climb without it.

But thirty years later, by proving that the oxygen lasted until they reached to the top, Bonatti cleared his name and thus rewrote the history of K2.

At 8,586 meters (28,169 feet), **KANCHENJUNGA** is the third highest mountain in the world. It has five peaks: its Nepali name translates as "the five treasures of the snow." One part of the mountain is in Nepal and the other part is in India.

On May 25, 1955, the British climbers, **George Band** and **Joe Brown** succeeded in reaching the top of Kanchenjungs but neither of them stood on the summit because the people of the Indian state Sikkim view the mountain peak as sacred.

At 8,516 meters (27,940 feet), **LHOTSE** is the fourth highest mountain on Earth. Always in the shadow of its imposing neighbor, Everest, Lhotse means "southern peak" in Tibetan.

On May 18, 1956, Swiss mountaineers **Ernst Reiss** and **Fritz Luchsinger** reached its summit for the first time.

At 8,463 meters (27,766 feet), **MAKALU** is the fifth highest mountain on Earth. It is located in the Himalayas and marks the border between Nepal and Tibet.

In 1955, French climber **Lionel Terray** and **Jean Couzy** were the first to reach the top. It is considered one of the most difficult mountains to climb in the world.

At 8,201 meters (26,906 feet), **CHO OYU** is the sixth highest mountain in the world.

On October 19, 1954, the Austrian expedition formed by **Herbert Tichy** and **Sepp Jöchler** reached its summit.

During that climb, the legendary **Pasang Dawa Lama**, one of the best *Sherpas* mountaineers of the 20th century, gained recognition.

At 8,167 meters (26,794 feet), **DHAULAGIRI** is the seventh highest peak on the planet. The name Dhaulagiri in Nepalese means "the white mountain."

The Austrian-Swiss expedition of **Kurt Diemberger, Peter Diener, Ernst Forrer, Albin Schelbert, Nyima Dorjee and Nawang Dorje** reached the summit for the first time on May 13, 1960.

On January 21, 1985, the Polish climbers **Jerzy Kukuczka** and **Andrzej Czok** successfully made the first winter ascent without using supplemental oxygen.

Located in the Himalayan mountain range in Nepal, at 8,156 meters (26,758 feet), **MANASLU** is the eighth highest mountain in the world.

On May 9, 1956, the Japanese climber **Toshio Imanishi** and Indian climber **Gyaltsen Norbu** were the first to reach the summit.

At 8,125 meters (26,657 feet), **NANGA PARBAT** is the ninth highest mountain in the world.

In 1953, the Austrian climber, **Hermann Buhl** became the only mountaineer to make the first ascent of an eight-thousander alone and without oxygen. So many climbers have died trying to reach the top, the mountain is nicknamed "the murderous mountain."

At 8,091 meters (26,545 feet), **ANNAPURNA** is the tenth highest mountain on the planet and the deadliest of the fourteen eight-thousanders.

With the help of a French expedition including **Gaston Rébuffat**, **Lionel Terray**, **Marcel Schatz**, **Jean Couzy**, **Jacques Oudot**, **Marcel Ichac** and **Francis de Noyelle**, on June 3, 1950, **Maurice Herzog** and **Louis Lachenal** summited Annapurna, the first eight-thousander to be climbed.

At 8,068 meters (26,470 feet), **GASHERBRUM I** is the eleventh highest peak on Earth.

July 5, 1958, American climbers **Pete Schoening** and **Andy Kaufman** made it to the top for the first time.

At 8,047 meters (26,401 feet), **BROAD PEAK** is the twelfth highest mountain on Earth and the fourth highest in Pakistan.

On June 9, 1957, an Austrian expedition with **Marcus Schmuck, Fritz Wintersteller, Kurt Diemberger** and **Hermann Buhl** were the first to successfully reach the summit.

At 8,035 meters (26,362 feet), **GASHERBRUM II**, in Pakistan, is the thirteenth highest mountain in the world.

In 1956, the Austrian climbers, **Sepp Larch**, **Fritz Moravec,** and **Hans Willempart** were the first to reach the top.

Located in the Tibet region, with its 8,027 meters (26,335 feet), **SIHSHAPANGMA** is the smallest of the fourteen summits that exceed eight thousand meters.

The Chinese mountaineer **Xu Jing** and nine other Tibetan mountaineers were the first to reach the summit in 1964.

Many of these feats would not have been possible without the help of *Sherpas*. *Sherpa* means "people of the East" which refers to the geographical region where most *Sherpas* live, which is eastern Tibet, in the eastern region of Nepal.

Sherpas are exposed to the greatest dangers on expeditions, because they are climbing guides in charge of preparing the route, opening the path, laying the ropes, loading the materials and removing all trash from the mountain.

Until the arrival of the first European expeditions at the beginning of the 20th century, almost all Sherpas were used to living in harsh weather conditions and at high altitudes. They were focused on agriculture rather than climbing.

Sherpa mountaineers hold numerous records. On January 6, 2021, the expedition consisting of **Sona Sherpa, Nirmal "Nims" Purja**, **Gelje Sherpa**, **Mingma David Sherpa**, **Mingma Tenzi Sherpa**, **Pem Chhiri Sherpa**, **Dawa Temba Sherpa**, **Mingma Gyalje Sherpa**, **Dawa Tenjing Sherpa** and **Kilu Pemba Sherpa**, ten Nepalese *Sherpas*, achieved the first winter ascent of K2.

Climate change is a reality: global warming and the continuing loss of glaciers are dramatically affecting the biodiversity of the eight-thousanders.

In addition, the rise in commercial expeditions in recent years is creating a serious pollution problem, as abandoned tents, food remains, and empty oxygen bottles accumulate on all the mountains.

The human impact on these ecosystems must be minimized by working together with the entire mountain community and the population that depends on mountain tourism. Sustainability and environmental management has to become important in order to preserve the ecology of these mountains.

EQUIPMENT

ROPE

The first ropes were made of hemp, but broke easily with the stress of a fall, so silk was added to help strengthen them. In 1948, nylon was introduced with the first braided synthetic rope. In 1952, a central core was added, using strings and an outer cover to protect climbers' hands from abrasion.

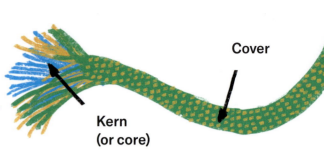

Cover

Kern (or core)

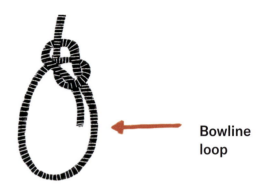

Bowline loop

AX

A tool that allows climbers to progress on snow slopes, carve steps, self-stop, and anchor themselves.

The ice ax is a small, short-handled tool with an ax and a hoe at the top.

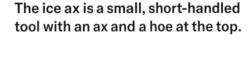

Then came the alpenstock, which increased the length to up to two meters (6 ½ feet) with a pickaxe at the top.

In 1840, the first prototype of a shorter (1 ½ meter/5 foot) ice ax was created by combining an ax and claw.

Around 1860, the ax head was elongated so the handle could be made shorter.

HARNESS

In the past, it was common to tie a harness to the body using knots such as the bowline.

In the 1960s, a wide ribbon tied at the waist, called a "swami," was used. It is a waist harness without legs.

In the 1970s, leg loops were added to the belt, creating the first modern harness.

SPIKE

Used in early mountaineering, but not used often by today's climbers, spikes require carrying a mallet or hammer to nail them into, and remove them from, a rock. Spikes can harm rocks if used too frequently.

JUMAR

In the 1950s, the Swiss climbers **Adolph Juesi** and **Walter Marti** invented the jumar, which is a mechanical device that allows you to ascend using a rope that locks when force is exerted.

CRAMPON

Metal cleats that can be attached to climbing boots to improve the grip for climbing or walking on ice or snow. In 1908, **Oscar Eckenstein** first commissioned the manufacture of a crampon from blacksmith **Henry Grivel** in a workshop in Courmayeur, Italy.

REVERSE

Until the middle of the 20th century, the way to belay (or secure a climber with a rope held by another person) was to pass a rope under the arm and tie it to the waist of the climber.

The first mechanical braking device appeared in 1970. Belay technology has continued to evolve through the invention of the reverse.

Reverses are devices for braking by using the friction on the rope.

FIGURE EIGHT

Before the appearance of the reverse, the main belay device was the figure eight. Currently it is only used when climbers are descending.

HELMET

At the end of the 1950s, the first prototypes of helmets appeared. In 1960, **August Schuster** marketed the first climbing helmet.

ICE SCREWS

A type of anchor used for ice belaying made of a threaded metal tube screwed into the ice by hand.

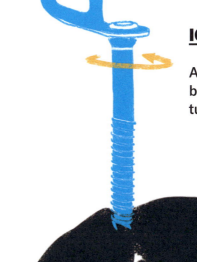

TRADITIONAL CLIMBING

In traditional or lead climbing, climbers use natural anchors whenever possible as well as artificial belays that the first person in the group places in fissures, cracks, and holes in the rock wall. The final climber of the group collects the artificial anchors and belays as they follow them up.

HISTORY

In 1911, Austrian mountaineer **Paul Preuss** changed climbing history forever. Faithful to a pure style, and without using anchors, the Alps were his playground. He succeeded in making more than a thousand historic climbs, many of them solo, which was something inconceivable with the rudimentary material of the time.

At the beginning of the 20th century, the German climber **Willo Welzenbach** made nearly a thousand difficult climbs and went down in history as the inspiration for a climbing grading table.

Another famous figure of this era was the Italian mountain guide and mountaineer **Angelo Dibona**. Considered one of the best climbers of the time, he was a pioneer of great climbs in the Alps and the Dolomites.

In the 1930s, breaking with the pure style of the time, the German climber, **Hans Dülfer** raised the difficulty levels. Using pitons, hooks, and ropes, he made more than fifty first ascents in the Alps. He was a pioneer in using compression and opposition when climbing.

26

At the same time, Italian climber, **Emilio Comici,** nicknamed "Angel of the Dolomites," was a star in that particular mountain range for making extremely difficult climbs.
In 1933, together with the the brothers **Angelo and Giuseppe Dimai,** he was the first to successfully climb the north face of the Cima Grande de Lavaredo.

Motivated by Comici's amazing climbs at the end of the 1930s, another of the great legends emerged: the Italian **Riccardo Cassin**. He achieved historic climbs in the Alps and the Himalayas.
In 1938, together with **Gino Esposito** and **Ugo Tizzoni**, he opened the Walker point of the Grandes Jorasses in the Mont Blanc group of mountains. Having worked as a blacksmith, he played a fundamental role in the evolution of climbing equipment.

During the 1950s and '60s, twin brothers wrote their name in the history books of the Pyrenees. The Frenchmen **Jean** and **Pierre Ravier** took classic climbing to another level.

And, in 1962 **Jean Ravier** was part of the first climb led by **Lionel Terray** of Jannu (7,710 meters or 25,925 feet), in the Himalayas.

The peaks in Yosemite National Park, in California, are considered to be the best group of great granite walls in the world. After the Second World War, Swiss climber **John Salathé** made his mark in Yosemite. He made historic first climbs, including the southwest face of Half Dome. The advances he made in the material of climbing gear changed this sport forever.

Royal Robbins was an important figure in Yosemite history. This creative mountaineer's respect for the rock and his elegant climbing technique are two standouts among his many achievements. The climb he made in 1961, with **Tom Frost** and **Chuck Pratt,** up the 9000-meter (29,528-feet) Salathé Wall was the most difficult route in the world at that time.

Warren Harding, achieved one of the greatest feats in the history of Yosemite on November 12, 1958, the first ascent of The Nose on El Capitan. He used an exceptionally large amount of climbing gear to get to the top, but made it.

In the seventies, during the psychedelic era and protests against the Vietnam War, **Jim Bridwell** led a new team of climbers in California, who became known as the **Stone Masters**. This group removed themselves from society, settled in the Camp 4 campground Yosemite, and took climbing to another level.

On May 26, 1975, **Jim Bridwell**, **John Long,** and **Billy Westbay** ascended the 3,000-foot (914 meter) Nose of El Capitan in a single day.

That same year, **John Bachar**, another of the key figures of the Stone Masters, climbed, together with **John Long** and **Ron Kauk**, the most difficult multi-pitch wall route in the world: "Astroman."

Of this legendary group of Yosemite Camp 4 climbers, one name would forever resonate in big wall history: American climber **Lynn Hill**.

After spending the 1980s climbing throughout Europe, Hill returned home to climb in Yosemite. Her achievements were incredible for any climber, but she is especially renowned for being the first woman to make the first free climb up The Nose of El Capitan in 1993. She is one of the most important figures in 20th-century climbing.

In 2015, American climbers **Tommy Caldwell** and **Kevin Jorgeson** went down in history by free climbing Yosemite's 900-meter Dawn Wall, the hardest big wall route in the world.

EQUIPMENT

CLIMBING SHOES

In the 1930s, the Italian mountaineer, **Vitale Bramani** invented the first vulcanized (hardened) rubber soles for mountain boots, the "**Vibram**" sole.

In 1935, the famous French climber, **Pierre Allain** created the first prototype for climbing shoes, the **PA**.

HELMET

REVERSE

The reverse tool was designed to simplify belay maneuvers, both for the first and second team members. It is also used for rappelling, making some of the maneuvers much easier.

HARNESS

MAGNESIUM

In the 1950s, American climber **John Gill** began using magnesium powder in climbing. By reducing hand moisture, climbers get a better grip.

DOUBLE ROPES

Double ropes are used to avoid friction as much as possible during climbing. Having two ropes also allows climbers to carry out long rappels by tying the ropes together. They are each lighter to carry than one long rope and each member of the team can carry one during the approach or descent, which shares the burden. They range between 7.8 and 8.9 millimeters in diameter, or about 1/3 inch.

CRACKS

Climbers use cracks in the rock for hand- and footholds.

In the fifties, bolts and pitons became commonly used. They were embedded in cracks to help climbers ascend the rocks where they could not get a handhold.

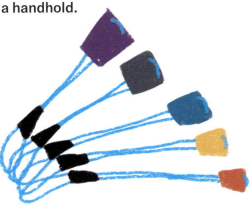

In the 1960s, **John Brailsford** designed the acorn or nut, which can be pre-threaded with a cord. Two years later, he invented the MOAC (a metal nut designed specifically for climbing).

WEBBING

Webbing is made of flat cords or ribbons that are used for making slings on rock bridges, or on the trees or bushes that grow out of the stone walls.

CLIMBING TAPE

HAMMOCK

Mountaineer **Mike Graham** invented the first prototype of a hammock that can be secured to a rock face or mountain, so climbers can sleep and rest on the large granite walls. It was First used in the 1980s on El Capitan, in Yosemite National Park.

COPPERHEAD

CORD

FRIEND

In the early seventies, the American climber **Ray Jardine** and the American climbing equipment manufacturer **Bill Forrest** created the first prototypes for a friend, a mechanism thatcompresses so it can be wedged into cracks and expand inside to provide security.

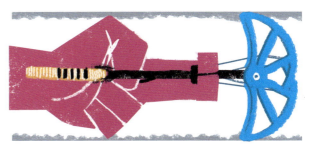

NAILS

CLIMBING PACK

31

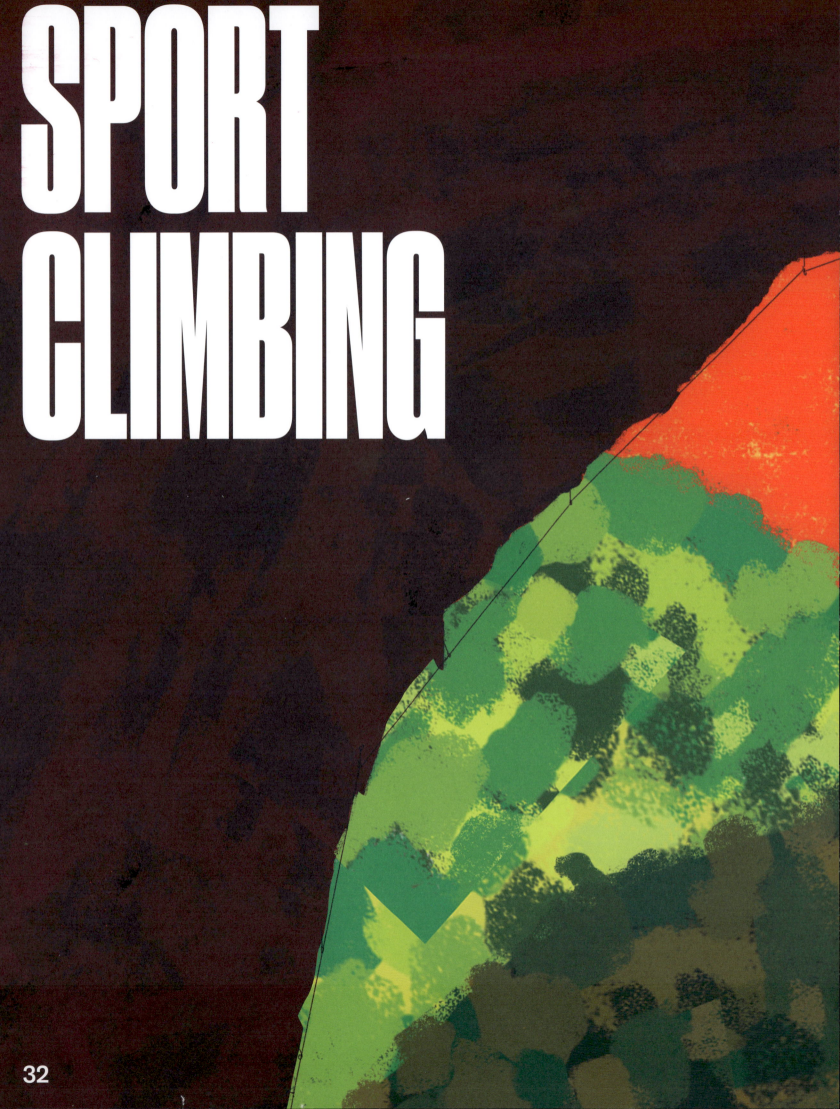
SPORT CLIMBING

This formof the sport allows climbers to use bolts that have already been placed in the rock, which is the opposite of traditional climbing.

In sport climbing, the routes have already been equipped with fixed safety devices. It appeals to those who want to climb but do not want to carry as much equipment and forge new trails.

HISTORY

In the 1970s, in spite of the disproval by traditional climbers, sport climbing developed in France and the United States. It soon began to spread to other countries as well.

In 1979, American sport climber **Toni Yaniro** climbed the world's most difficult sport climbing route, Grand Illusion, in California.

He was able to cross one leg over his arm to take a long step. That move is now known as "the Yaniro movement."

Although it is not widely used among rock climbers, it is commonly used by ice climbers.

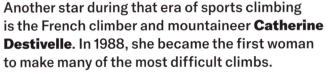

Patrick Edlinger revolutionized French climbing in the seventies and eighties. With his fluid climbing style, he was a key figure in the birth of sport climbing.

Another star during that era of sports climbing is the French climber and mountaineer **Catherine Destivelle**. In 1988, she became the first woman to make many of the most difficult climbs.

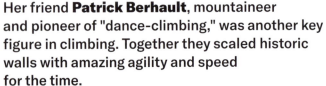

Her friend **Patrick Berhault**, mountaineer and pioneer of "dance-climbing," was another key figure in climbing. Together they scaled historic walls with amazing agility and speed for the time.

In the mid-1980s, French climbers, **Jibé Tribout** and brothers **Marc** and **Antoine Le Menestrel** raised the difficulty bar for sport climbing in the town of Buoux, France.

For many the best climber in the 1980s was the British climber **Jerry Moffatt**.
A tireless traveler, he succeeded in making several historic first ascents in Europe, the United States, and Africa.

In 1989, his traveling companion, English climber **Ben Moon,** raised the level by climbing Agincourt, in Buoux. The mountain's name, Agincourt, is a reference to England's victory over France in the Hundred Years' War, in 1415.

Without a doubt, another legendary figure from this period was the German climber **Wolfgang Güllich.** He was one of the pioneers during the eighties and nineties. In 1991, he climbed the most difficult route in the history of sport climbing up to that point, Action Directe, in Frankenjura, Germany.

His friend and teammate, the revolutionary German climber **Kurt Albert**, coined the term *redpoint.* Redpointing is lead climbing a route to the top without falling or resting on the rope, after failing in a previous attempt.

37

At the end of the 1980s, the young Japanese climber **Yuji Hirayama** became known as a versatile climber in all disciplines. In 1989, he opened the ascent to Flat Mountain, one of the toughest routes in Japan. In 1998 and 2000, he won the Difficulty Climbing World Cup.

In the 1990s, German mountaineer **Alex Huber** raised the level of difficulty even further by opening one of the most difficult routes of the time, La Rambla, in the Tarragona town of Siurana, Spain.

Also in Siurana, in 2013, the young nineteen-year-old German climber **Alex Megos** wrote his name in climbing history by successfully climbing Critical State onsight, the highest grade climbed onsight so far.

Onsight climbing is climbing a route, on the first attempt, without falling, without help, and without knowing anything about the route.

In 1998, the Austrian climber **Beat Kammerlander** equipped the two hundred and fifty meters of the WoGü route, named after **Wolfgang Güllich**, in the Rätikon mountain group in Switzerland. It has several of the most difficult pitches in the world.

In 2005, the Spanish climber **Josune Bereziartu** made history by completing the second ascent of Bimbaluna, in Saint Loup, Switzerland, one of the most difficult in the world.

38

The legendary American climber **Chris Sharma** won the US Open Bouldering Nationals for adults at the age of fourteen. In 1997, at sixteen, he placed second at the World Championships in Paris.

He then stopped competing and dedicated himself to traveling in search of routes with the highest difficulty and greatest beauty.

In 2001, Sharma made history by being the first to ascend the legendary forty-meter sports climbing route of Biographie, in Céüse, France. It was a milestone at that time.

But if anyone has broken all the records in all disciplines, it is the young Czech climber **Adam Ondra**. Many consider him to be the best sports climber in history.

At the age of thirteen he was already climbing top-grade routes. In 2014, he won the World Bouldering Championships and the World Difficulty Climbing Championships. He has climbed more than two hundred high-difficulty routes.

In 2017, he made climbing history by ascending Silence, the world's most difficult sports climbing route to date, in Flatanger, Norway.

EQUIPMENT

HARNESS

HELMET

ROPE

In sport climbing, a simple dynamic rope (a rope with some stretch) is used, designed to absorb and cushion the fall.

CLIMBING SHOE

In the early 1980s, the Spanish company Boreal invented a rubber sole that improved grip.

MAGNESIUM

40

BELAY

Protects the lead climber from falling.

PACK

REVERSE DEVICE

BELAY PLATE

The plate is a metal safety element with a hole in the center that is screwed to the rock to equip climbing routes. The anchor line is a rope attached to the harness at one end to anchor the climber to the belay before making the descent maneuver.

QUICKDRAWS

Until the mid-20th century, only a carabiner was used. Quickdraws improve the bond between the anchor and the rope. They consist of two carabiners joined by a sewn strap.

Straight trigger, a more dynamic carabiner for anchoring to the wall.

CARABINER

Until the late 1930s, carabiners were made of iron. In 1939, French mountaineer **Pierre Allain** invented the first aluminum carabiners.

In sport climbing, carabiners are used with the belay or belay mount.

ANCHOR

The safest anchors are composed of a stainless-steel rod and resin.

Curved trigger and static carabiner through which the rope is passed.

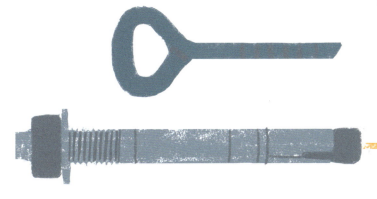

PARABOLT

The parabolt is a fixed anchor with an expansion system. It has a thread where a nut and a washer are placed to fix the sheet.

SHEET

The sheet is a metal safety element with a hole in the center that can be screwed to the rock to equip climbing routes.

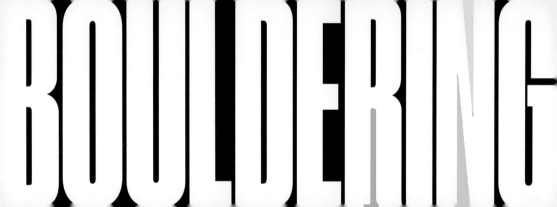

Bouldering is a form of free climbing rock formations or rock walls that are no more than twenty feet.

It requires a smaller number of movements and requires climbers to use technical and explosive steps.

HISTORY

In 1870, Parisian climbers traveled to Fontainebleau, France, to prepare physically and technically on different circuits before embarking on their climbing expeditions.

In the following decade, the famous mountaineer **Oscar Eckenstein** and his friend **Aleister Crowley** became pioneers of bouldering, which uses movements typical of gymnastics to ascend boulders.

In the 1930s, Frenchman **Pierre Allain**, one of the most important climbers in pre-war France, joined the historic group of young climbers called the **Bleausards**, who were pioneers of bouldering in Fontainebleau.

In the 1950s, American **John Gill**, considered by many to be the father of bouldering, combined gymnastics moves with climbing. In 1961, Gill managed to climb The Thimble in Custer State Park South Dakota, a thirty-foot wall that no one was able to scale again for decades.

In 1978, American **Ron Kauk** climbed Midnight Lightning in Yosemite, the greatest bouldering challenge of the time. In 1998, **Lynn Hill** became the first woman to scale it. A member of Hill's climbing group **John Bachar** designed a magnesium-painted lightening bolt as an icon of free climbing, based on a Jimi Hendrix song.

In the mid-1980s, the French climber **Jacky Godoffe** drawn by the beauty of the area, was the first to repeat the success of climbing the most difficult boulders of Fontainebleau.

In the 1980s and 90s, two outstanding figures in bouldering were the British climbers **Ben Moon** and **Jerry Moffatt**. Also before legendary figures in sport climbing, they succeeded in making the first ascents of the hardest routes of the time. They had an important role in the development of bouldering and training.

The climber who changed the history of bouldering at the beginning of the 21st century is the Swiss climber **Fred Nicole**. A tireless traveler, he opened legendary extreme routes in Rocklands (South Africa), Hueco Tanks (Texas) and Cresciano (Switzerland).

In 2005, American climber **Chris Sharma** became the first to make it to the top of Witness the Fitness, which is one of the toughest challenges in America. That same year, fellow American **Dave Graham** continued to increase the challenge of the sport by climbing The Story of Two Worlds, in Cresciano, Switzerland.

In 2015, fourteen-year-old American **Ashima Shiraishi** attained the highest bouldering grade by climbing Nuclear War, in Harriman Park, New York.

Another climber addicted to the extreme difficulty of bouldering is the Czech climber **Adam Ondra**. In 2020, he made the first ascent of Brutal Rider, the toughest challenge in the Czech Republic.

In 2016, the Finnish climber **Nalle Hukkataival** raised the degree of difficulty of bouldering to new levels by climbing Burden of Dreams, in Lappnor, Finland.

In 2019, American climber **Nina Williams** succesfullyu ascended the extremely difficult Too Big To Flail, in Bishop, California.

MATERIAL

CAT FEET

BRUSH

MAGNESIUM

CRASHPAD

The **crashpad** (or bouldering mat) is a mat that is placed on the ground to cushion falls.

SOLO

Solo climbers scale boulders and rock walls without ropes, harnesses, or other protective equipment.

In 1986, the German climber **Wolfgang Güllich** made the first solo climb of Separate Reality, a route 200 meters (656 feet) high in Yosemite Valley.

In 1987, the French climber **Catherine Destivelle** solo climbed 500 meters (1640 feet) on the Cliffs of Bandiagara, in Mali.

On June 3, 2017, American climber **Alex Honnold** made history by solo climbing the 914 meters (3000 feet) of El Capitan, in Yosemite National Park.

On February 22, 2015, climber and American mountaineer **Brette Harrington** solo climbed 750 meters (2461 feet) of Chiaro di Luna, in the Fitz Roy range, Patagonia.

FREE BASE

Free base unites two disciplines, solo climbing and the base jump. It consists of solo climbing with a parachute. Then, at a certain height, the climber does a base jump.

On August 6, 2008, the American climber **Dean Potter** completed the first free-base ascent of the 300 meters (984 feet) high Deep Blue Sea, in the face north of the Eiger, Switzerland.

URBAN CLIMBING

Solo urban climbing consists of climbing buildings, monuments, bridges, and other structures without ropes or safety equipment.

The greatest expert of urban climbing is the French climber **Alain Robert**. Known as the "French Spiderman," he is famous for solo climbing skyscraper all over the world.

PSICOBLOC

Psicobloc consists of climbing rock walls without a rope above water at a minimum height of 15 to 20 meters (60-65 feet). In the 1980s, the Spanish climber **Miquel Riera** (who many consider the father of psychobloc) developed this discipline in his native Mallorca and then took it to new levels of difficulty.

In the 2020 Tokyo Olympic Games, climbing was included for the first time in history as an Olympic sport. Twenty climbers competed in three disciplines.

SPEED CLIMBING

Climbers compete to be the fastest to reach the top on identical tracks on a 15 meters (50-foot) wall.

BOULDERING

Climbers scale 15 feet (4.5 meter) walls without ropes, in a limited period of time and in the fewest attempts possible.

LEAD CLIMBING

In the lead event, athletes climb as high as they can on a wall over 15 meters (50 feet) high in six minutes, without having seen the route ahead of time.

For the women's climbing event, the gold medal was awarded to Slovenian climber **Janja Garnbret,** the silver went to Japanese climber **Miho Nonaka,** and the bronze was won by **Akiyo Noguchi.**

The gold medal for men went to Spanish climber **Alberto Ginés,** the silver medal went to American **Nathaniel Coleman,** and the bronze was awarded to Austrian climber **Jakob Schubert**.

CLIMBING WALLS

When climbing walls were invented, the holds were made of carved wood or brick. The next generation of holds were made of resin, and now polyurethane is used to create the holds.

Climbing walls were created at the end of the 1930s as small rooms whose function was to train for rock climbing.

PARACLIMBING

Paraclimbing is a climbing form designed for people with disabilities.

In 2011, the first World Cup Paraclimbing Championship was organized in Arco, Italy.

The nature of each athlete's disability is considered when designing events.

Some stand out climbs were made by blind British climber **Jesse Dufton** as well as by **Thomas Meier**, a German climber, and **Urko Carmona**, a Spanish climber, both of whom had only one leg.

ROCK DAMAGE

In the past, grips have altered the natural rock as climbers have secured anchors to help them get safely to the top. Unfortunately, even today there are those who continue to damage the rock with carvings, chopping, and using spikes to ascend a boulder or wall. It is vital to be aware of our footprint and to respect the natural forms of the rock.

HUMAN WASTE

It is now common to find poop, paper, and wipes near climbing areas. In addition to the time it takes to decompose, those remains contaminate nearby water and endanger the native animals.

The best way to get rid of poop is to use a shovel or a rake, make a hole about eight inches deep and bury it to speed it up its decomposition.

MAGNESIUM

Excessive use of magnesium can be harmful. When finished, it is important to clean and brush the magnesium marks left on the rock, both to respect the environment and to not confuse other climbers.

TRASH

It is essential to care for the environment and to pick up all the trash we either create or find while climbing.

THE PIONEERS

The creation of this book would have been impossible without the pioneers who ventured into the unknown to find the first climbers who knew how to find the precise path in the middle of a great wall.

Thank you also to the outfitters who have spent time and money on plotting beautiful climbing routes.

To all of them, thank you.

GLOSSARY

ACORN (see nut)

AID CLIMBING a type of climbing that makes use of rope, fixed bolts, pitons, or foot slings, rather than features on the rock itself, to ascend the face.

ALPENSTOCK a specialized ax up to two meters (6 1/2 feet) in length with a pickaxe at the top.

ANCHOR a point of attachment for a climbing rope, usually made of stainless steel.

AXE (also climbing axe or pick axe) A tool that allows climbers to progress on snow slopes, carve steps, self-stop, and anchor themselves.

BELAY a system that stops a climber's fall. It includes the rope, anchors, belay device, and the belayer. Belay plate—a small metal sheet with a hole in the center that is screwed to the rock to equip climbing routes.

BELAYER the person who manages the rope to stop the lead climber if they fall.

BOLTED ROUTE a route with pre-placed bolt anchors rather than removable protection pieces. A sport route.

BOLTS metal expansion bolts drilled into the rock for use as protection for climbers.

BOULDERING climbing close to the ground without the use of a rope. Typically used for practicing traverses, weight transfers, and foot and hand placements. Can be done on boulders or at the base of a rock face.

CAMMING rotating protective gear into place until wedged or tight.

CAMMING DEVICE a piece of climbing protection that wedges into a crack by rotating.

CARABINER a metal loop (usually aluminum) with a spring-loaded gate on one side used for connecting various parts of a climbing system.

CAT FEET bouldering shoes.

CHALK (see magnesium)

CLIMBER a person who participates in the sport of climbing.

CLIMBING ascending rock, snow, ice, or walls.

COPPERHEAD a small nut with a loop of wire that can be placed in shallow seams and used as a grip.

CORD a short climbing rope used for many purposes in climbing.

CORE the center fibers of a climbing rope. Climbing tape—athletic tape used to protect hands and fingers while climbing.

CRACK a fissure in a rock wall, typically used for hand- and footholds while climbing.

CRAMPON metal cleats that can be attached to climbing boots to improve grip for climbing or walking on ice or snow.

FACE the sheer part of a cliff.

FIGURE 8 a climbing knot tied in the shape of the number 8, typically used for tying the climbing rope to the climber's harness. Also, the name of a rappel tool in the same shape.

FREE BASE unites two disciplines, solo climbing and the base jump. It consists of solo climbing with a parachute. Then, at a certain height the climber does a base jump.

FREE CLIMBING to climb using only hands and feet on the rock. Rope is used only for safety and is not relied upon for upward progress.

FREE SOLO climbing without a belay, which is often high risk. Unlike bouldering, free soloing goes far above the ground on full-length routes (see Solo climbing).

FRIEND a spring-loaded camming device.

HAMMOCK a climbing hammock that can be secured to the side of a rock face or mountain.

HARNESS a belt-and-leg-loop system that attaches a climber to a rope. Usually a seat harness is used for rock climbing.

ICE AXE a small, short-handled tool with an ax and a hoe at the top.

ICE-CLIMBING using specific equipment such as ice tools and crampons to ascend ice or snow fields.

ICE SCREW an anchor used for ice belaying made of a threaded metal tube screwed into the ice by hand.

JUMAR the original mechanical ascender, it is a mechanical device that allows you to ascend using a rope that locks when force is exerted.

LEAD the first person on a climb, either clipping the rope into bolts or placing protection for the other climbers.

MAGNESIUM chalk used to keep a climber's hands dry for better grip.

NUT a wedge-shaped piece of metal affixed to a wire that can be secured as a protection piece. Originally modeled after railway nuts.

MOUNTAINEERING the sport of climbing to the summit of mountain peaks.

ON SIGHT to lead a climb in the first attempt without falling and with no prior knowledge of the route.

OPENER the climber who affixes permanent protective gear to a climbing route.

PACK a gear bag for climbers.

PARABOLT a fixed anchor with an expansion system. It has a thread where a nut and a washer are placed to fix the sheet.

PARACLIMBING a climbing form designed for people with disabilities.

PITON a thin, wedge-like piece of metal that is pounded into a rock face and then clipped to the climbing rope for protection. The original means of protecting climbs, now out of favor because of the damage it does to the rock.

PROTECTION any device used to secure a climbing rope to rock, snow, or ice to prevent a climber from falling any significant distance.

PSICOBLOC climbing rock walls without a rope above water at a minimum height 15 to 20 meters (60-65 feet).

QUICKDRAW a short runner used to attach a rope to a bolted anchor with carabiners.

RAPPEL to descend a cliff or other height by lowering oneself on a fixed rope, with feet against the wall.

REDPOINT (OR RED POINT) to lead a climb without falling or putting weight on the rope, regardless of number of attempts. Applies to difficult climbs.

REVERSE device for braking by using the friction on the rope, designed to simplify belay maneuvers, both for the first and second team members.

ROUTE the path or moves up a specific climb.

SHEET a metal safety element with a hole that can be screwed to the rock to equip climbing routes.

SHERPAS climbing guides in charge of preparing the route, opening the path, laying the ropes, loading the material, and removing trash from the mountain.

SINGLE ROPE a rope whose diameter is large enough to support a leader fall when used singly.

SOLO CLIMBING to climbing alone without protection.

SPEED CLIMBING a competition that tests how far a climber can progress in a given time or how long it takes to complete a given climb.

SPIKE used in early mountaineering, but not used often by today's climbers, spikes require carrying a mallet or hammer to nail them into and remove them from the rock. Spikes can harm rock if used too frequently.

SPORT CLIMBING rock climbing using pre-placed protection such as bolts or a top rope. Frequently involves difficult, gymnastic moves. Opposite of traditional climbing.

TRADITIONAL CLIMBING also called lead climbing. Climbers use natural anchors whenever possible and artificial belays that the first person in the group places in fissures, cracks, and holes in the rock wall. The final climber of the group collects the anchors as they follow them up.

TRIGGER a carabiner.

URBAN CLIMBING climbing buildings, monuments, bridges, and other structures without ropes or safety equipment.

WEBBING woven nylon tape used for making slings and runners for climbing. It can also be used on trees and rock bridges.